MUSE

MUSE

poems from early motherhood

SARAH GRAHAM

'Words are, in my not-so-humble opinion,
our most inexhaustible source of magic.'
J.K. Rowling

'A mother's love for her child is like nothing else in the world. It knows no law, no pity. It dares all things and crushes down remorselessly all that stands in its path.'
Agatha Christie

'Give sorrow words; the grief that does not speak knits up the over-wrought heart, and bids it break."
Shakespeare

Published by matrescent muse

Copyright © Sarah Graham 2023

All rights reserved. This book or parts thereof may not be reproduced in any form or transmitted in any form by any means—electronic, mechanical, photocopy, recording, or otherwise, except in the case of brief quotations for the purpose of book reviews.

The perspectives represented in this book are those of the author only.

Book cover and interior design by Teresa Prowse.

Printed by Ingram Lightning Source.

This book and the poems within were created on the unceded lands of the Ngunnawal people of the ACT region in Australia. The author pays respect to the rich knowledge, traditions and stories of the Ngunnawal people and acknowledges their continuing cultural practices around motherhood and birth.

ISBN: 9780646885988 (paperback).

www.matrescentmuse.com
@matrescentmuse

Contents

1	**Introduction**		
5	**The Early Days**		
		Homecoming	6
		Language of the Heart	7
		Incredible	8
		Whole	10
		Transformed	11
		Two Hearts	15
		Free Flow	16
		Our Love is Heavy	18
		The Push and Pull	20
		Spring Rivers	24
		To Me, the Newborn Mother	25
		Nightcall	29
		The Spectre	31
33	**Matrescence**		
		Sun, Moon and Stars	34
		The Pendulum	35
		Baby's Poem	36
		Evening Prayer	38
		Dear Old Me	40
		Call You Mine	45
		On Air	46
		Coexist	47
		Golden Honey	49
		Full Circle	51

	Love Her Like You	54
	Some Days	58
	If It Weren't for You	59
	The Moon and the Tide	63
	Growing	66
	I Go to You	67
	Paradox	68
	Do Not Tell Me	69
74	**Grief, Life and Loss**	
	Our Friend Up In The Stars	75
	No More Will We Feed	77
	Back to the Rocking Chair	80
	The Angels	83
	In Every Lifetime	85
	'Til The End	86
	A Love That Was Like No Other	90
92	**Friends and Lovers**	
	Simple Privilege	93
	Dear Mum	94
	In the Trenches	98
	To Our Shore	100
	Note to My Love	101
	To My Darling	103
107	**Poems from the Pandemic**	
	In the Year that I Was Born	108
	Pandemic Poem	112
	To The Locked-Down Mums	114
117	**Acknowledgements**	
119	**About the Author**	

Introduction

I had always expected that becoming a mother would change me, though I could never have expected the scale of that transformation.

When I think back to the initial weeks after my first baby arrived, the memories are a saturated blur of pain, exhaustion and overwhelming love. My husband and I were flooded with many moments of happiness and wonder as we processed the sheer fact of our little one's existence.

Our earliest days together - and some months afterward - were also marked by an extremely challenging start to breastfeeding. I had entered motherhood with the naive assumption that because I was keen to breastfeed, I would simply do so, and that was that. The birth was supposed to have been the challenge; once the baby had arrived, I thought, we would spend our days feeding together in easy, instinctive bliss.

It came as a rude shock, therefore, when breastfeeding revealed itself to be the most excruciating experience I had ever endured. The pain was a bloody, teeth-gritting, toe-curling torture that existed within a relentless cycle. Devoted to the idea of nourishing my daughter with my body, yet fearing the pain that it would inflict, I felt like a disciple determined to self-flagellate for a holy cause. The three-or-so-hourly approach of feeding time was regularly anticipated with dread.

Between those difficult feeds, however, another feeling began to emerge—one that was almost the emotional antithesis to the pain of breastfeeding. It was a swooping feeling in my chest, a flutter, a lump in the throat, a feeling of hope, and hopelessness, of joy and wonder, of deepest devotion and pure, overflowing joy. I can picture sitting beside her in the back seat of the car, the way her perfect and impossibly-tiny frame looked in the car seat. She was here, I thought; she was real, and our time together was already ticking away. On one hand, I couldn't believe she existed, and yet on the other I felt all-too-aware of the fact that she was changing before my eyes. I wanted to hold her, to freeze that moment in time, and yet longed to know who she would grow to be, to watch her thrive in this world.

This sensation, of course, was love—bursting with highs and lows, encompassing me and unravelling me. It was a love I had never felt before, a love like no other—a Mother's love.

These overwhelming emotional states coloured those first few weeks. We were tired, sore, happy and complete. Yet new motherhood was still unfolding for me, and the feelings of change continued to come in new and different waves.

Around the time that my husband returned to work, and our family visitors had returned to their interstate homes, another feeling overcame me. This was a different sensation to pain, or exhaustion, or love. Our daughter was going through a long period in which she would only contact-nap. I had been sitting on the lounge, pinned beneath her sleeping form for hours, when this new feeling seemed to dawn on me heavily.

Introduction

My old life, I suddenly felt, was gone. Everything that I had been able to do before she was born seemed to exist in a past life. It was as thought the girl that I had once been, with her autonomy, her freedom and simplicity, had died, and in her place was me, the mother: a wan and lifeless shadow. Pinned beneath my baby's tiny form, I sat very still, fearing to even move a muscle should I wake her. I needed the toilet, I needed a drink of water, yet anxiety built in me and I dared not face the stress of resettling my baby if I put her down. Suddenly, my future seemed to lay itself out in front of me, a never-ending cycle of routine in a lifetime of 'groundhog days'. I pictured myself even a few months prior, when I moved about freely, unaware of the simple freedoms that I had possessed before she came into my life.

I knew that I loved my baby, and would never change her existence for the world. She was the most beautiful life-giving joy we had ever witnessed - of that I was sure. Yet there, tethered to the lounge, alone and silent, I still cried and mourned deeply for a life and identity that I couldn't remember signing over.

In time, I would learn that there was a term for what I was experiencing—matrescence—the process of transformation as a mother enters and navigates the new role, identity and existence that motherhood brings. With time, too, I came to see this role in a new light. This transition had rocked me, and yet had taken me somewhere very precious.

As the shock of this transition eased, and I settled into my new role, I realised that the girl I had been had not died after all. I regained small freedoms, and parts of my identity resurfaced so that I began to recognise myself again. Even if my weary fourth-trimester-brain had once believed it impossible, I did, of course, regain the freedom to empty my bladder and get a glass of water at will (albeit, at times, with uninvited company). I found pockets of time to do the things that had made me feel like 'me'. True, I wasn't quite 'that girl' anymore, but she had not disappeared completely. The core of who I was remained the same, yet out of that core I had expanded, shifted and gained new strength—born out of the struggles I had thought I was incapable of enduring.

Becoming a mother has changed me beyond recognition, and I have no doubt that this process is not over. It has brought me joy, pain, despair, beauty, and inconceivable love. It is bright and warm and light, and at some times, lonely and dark. Yet, as many mothers might say, it is a blessing that I wouldn't trade for those freedoms I once enjoyed. I picture my little daughter's sweet, beautiful, silly little face, and I just want to squeeze her, kiss her and never let her go—much like my hold on being a mother.

Early motherhood is kaleidoscopic, and I have attempted to reflect this beautiful and chaotic period here in these poems, with the hopes that they might bring comfort to another mother.

Sarah

The Early Days

Homecoming

Mumma, you don't know me yet,
But I already know you;
Your voice, your scent, the way you move,
And everything you do

For months, I've felt your heartbeat,
Heard you humming absently,
I know your laugh, I've heard your cries
And sweet words whispered to me

So when we meet, it might seem like
You're greeting someone new -
But Mumma, I'll be coming home,
For my home was always you.

The Early Days

Language of the Heart

In the early days you'll wonder
How to translate it all into a text message:
How your body is still contracting,
Leaking, bleeding,
How you didn't sleep last night
And the feeding is such agony, you
Can't even bear the thought of it;
How every day, you ask yourself whether
Is it possible to mourn the life you once knew,
While living in awe of a new one?
A new being,
Whose divine and delicate features
(The same ones that you felt moving in you)
Are finally here before you, and oh, so real -
YOU made them, from scratch!
And the crushing reality of their very existence
Is in equal parts tender, sweet and pure,
And you think that
You might just be
Falling in love?

So for now, you send a picture of the baby,
Tell them, "Thanks, we're doing well."
For a mother's love exists not
In the words we know,
But in the language of the heart.

Incredible

Others told me
Of their amazing babies,
The lucky ones,
The 'unicorn' ones
Who went to sleep all on their own,
Found comfort in the surface of their cot,
Never woke,
Never needed help in the night

"That's incredible," I whispered,
My voice feeble in the wonder and the
Disbelief and the envy.
I imagined their freedom,
Their blissful rest,
The ownership they must have felt over
Their own body -
How had they already reclaimed
So much of the life that
I was mourning?

Months later
You still call for me in the night
Cries echoing through corridors,
Craving for us to be close.
I drag myself from bed,
Wearing my resentment in layers thick and heavy,
Bleary-eyed, staggering half in sleep.

Yet the truth is
What happens next is magic.

The Early Days

How is it, that in a moment, your shuddering cries are stilled
By my smell, my arms?
As though you're returning home to a
Place you've known since your were born
And your little sobs slow to deep inhalations
As though you are breathing me in, and thinking
"Thank goodness,
She heard me,
I know who this is -
This is *her*."

And somehow, just as I soothed you,
You play your sacred part in this symbiosis

Your tiny hand, so soft I can hardly feel it
Traces across my skin,
And like a wand, spreads warmth through me
Lighting my soul with love,
Thawing a tightness in me
Until all resentment fades
And we are enshrined there,
Cocooned in love, cloaked by the night,
A magic as old as life.

And in the dark and bliss
I think to myself,
This is incredible.

Whole

My body came apart to bring you here,
And so did my soul
Both were stitched and swollen
And both still bled
And slowly the 'me' that was, leaked away
From where they both were torn.

Each day I put them back together
Ice and pads,
Pills and heat packs,
But the sweetest anaesthetic was your love:

You licked my wounds just by being,
And though the pain came from
Bringing you here,
So too were you the remedy:
Ancient elixir,
Sacred salve,
You made me whole again.

The Early Days

Transformed

A friend said: "You'll never be the same"
You answered, "You're right, I'm sure."
After all, you weren't completely naive
About what you were in for:
The feeding, the nappies, the lack of sleep
Life changed in a permanent way;
You knew that you would be on-call
For twenty-four hours a day

They wished you all the very best,
But their smile was hard to read -
You gave a nervous laugh, and thought,
How bad is it going to be?
And yes, the first few nights were rough
Once your baby was finally born:
Love and exhaustion, cuddles and tears -
You were tired, sore and torn

But as days passed in that newborn blur
A strange new sensation emerged,
It made you feel giddy, teary and sick
Yet caused your heart to surge
It wasn't about it being hard work,
It was different altogether -
An epiphany, a reverie
Transforming you forever

And at that very moment
A switch was flicked in you -
Changing you deep within your core,
It was something entirely new
You held their tiny days-old form
Wishing the moment would linger,
As you suddenly, desperately felt that time
Was slipping through your fingers

Would you remember them being so small?
The size of their tiny toes?
The way that a sneeze could shake their whole frame,
The lines from a yawn on their nose -
You studied their features, their image etched
Upon your heart like a brand -
For the photos could not quite capture the weight
Of their body laid in your hands

And you realised that what you knew of "love"
Had swelled to infinity
The miracle of their perfect form,
Mother Nature's divinity
You watched them sleep and you knew right then
That angels could be real
And as you cried, your soul rejoiced
With a whole new capacity to feel

The Early Days

And paired with the love was a knowledge, too,
Terrible enough to disarm:
Though life would bring them love and joy,
It would also cause them harm
You sobbed into your partner's chest:
"What if someone is mean to them?"
And you squashed any thoughts of other things,
Too dark to even imagine

For this love was ingrained with a burden,
Its own vulnerability:
Your fierce desire to keep them safe
Had a sense of futility
You'd protect them with all of your power, but knew
That one day you'd need to surrender -
And the tears were a premature mourning
For the way that the world would affect them

Later, you saw that friend again
She asked you how you were
And though this feeling you wanted to share,
You couldn't quite find the words:
How could you explain that your heart had grown
To be ten-times the size?
That your giver of life was no longer the sun,
That the universe lived in their eyes?
That you knew you'd created something divine,
Yet like all beings, was fragile still,
And protecting them felt an impossible task,
A mission you couldn't fulfil?

You broke from your thoughts, noticing
Your friend was watching you.
You didn't have to speak at all -
You could tell that they just 'knew'.
They had said, "You'll never be the same"
And you realised, they were right:
This love had set your soul aflame,
And made your heart ignite

As fierce as it was tender,
Both ancient and still new,
A love that was formidable
Yet gentle, sweet and true
And though the thoughts of years to come
Weighed heavy on your brow
You released them gently, content to simply
Hold her, just for now.

The Early Days

Two Hearts

I remember when I had two hearts
Beating within me, quiet
In their steady rhythm,
One yours, one mine
And now your arms reach and
You cry out for them to be near again,
Wriggling against me 'til every gap is filled,
'Til your heart is pressed close against mine and
Your eyes grow heavy.
So I'll hold you close,
Even though the books tell me I should put you down,
Even as time moves past us
Because I know that somehow, we're still the same -
You, an extension of me -
I still have two hearts,
One yours, one mine.

'Two Hearts' was the first poem I wrote about motherhood.

Free Flow

I used to hate it
I'd scream and cry
Beg your dad for something to bite down on,
Bang my fist on the arm of the chair
'Til he'd scoop you up and
Carry you away
Your tiny head bobbing over his shoulder,
Crying for something that brought me a pain
Worse than bringing you into the world
And me, a crumpled heap
Defeated, insufficient,
Guilty.

We tried to solve it

Every resource, every appointment,

Every trick -

But we were two puzzle pieces that

Didn't seem to fit.

So for weeks I watched the clock,

Dreading every feed.

How could something so natural be so hard?

I was lucky, the nurses said -

I had plenty of milk

And it flowed as freely as my tears

Whenever you tried to drink it,

Nurturing you in my agony.

The Early Days

Weeks later we watched the sunrise over the ocean
A band of crimson on blue
And I realised the pain was fading
And for the first time, I was able to watch you
Peaceful, rhythmic, sweet
Your eyes wide and trusting,
Something ancient about it
A connection - between us,
Between all the women before us
The puzzle pieces that fit
And I pictured the smiles of those who had
Promised me it would get better,
Because they were right.
And the tears flowed again
But this time, with no pain.

Our Love is Heavy

Before, I was more free than I knew.
My own person, my own time,
My own body
Now, that freedom is filled
With the euphoric, heaving,
Magic, tender,
Blissful and crushing weight
Of you.

And would I go back, if I could?
To swap the glances at the clock for
Being on no one's time?
The weight of your little body
For one comfortable night in bed?
To forget the dragging on my heart
From a cry that won't be soothed
To be alone without the pressing feeling
That my seconds are numbered -
A rushed shower, each minute
Disappearing down the drain -
And soon, I'll need to do it all over
And over
And over and over again.

The Early Days

And I wonder, was it right?
To bring you into this life
where a border separates us from the help I crave,
The people I love,
The ones you barely know.
We lay feeding in the dark
I stifle my sobs -
You're so distractible lately -
But you hear me,
Breaking away to look up.
Wide eyed, milky smile.

I bow my head
My lips brushing through your precious hair
to kiss your tiny forehead
And my breath catches in my throat,
And the heaviness is lifted
By that smile - pure, perfect joy,
And I know that I love you more than
Anything in the universe.
I'm bound to you.
It's heavy, this love,
Because it is so full.

The Push and Pull

On Day Two, we brought you home
We spent the whole night awake
Broken, exhausted; we asked ourselves,
"Have we made an awful mistake?"
You cried in a language so foreign to us,
And my heart breaks in hindsight to see
That all you wanted, all that you craved
Was to spend the night close to me

Yet I had done all of the reading on sleep,
Your bassinet firm and bare,
But whenever we placed you inside, you cried
For something that wasn't there
My warmth, my smell; my heartbeat had been
The soundtrack of your rest
So now, the place that you wanted to sleep
Was against me, chest to chest

The Early Days

And so for weeks, you lived in my arms
Never wanting to sleep alone
And the price that was paid was my freedom,
The 'me' that I once had known
At night we brought you into our bed,
Breaking all of the rules we'd been told -
Guilty, and yet cocooned in bliss,
While your bassinet still remained cold

And it mostly stayed a secret,
For we knew it wasn't safe
And yet it felt so natural;
My arms, your sacred place
And after all, we'd toiled so long
To settle you on your own -
For hours we tried to soothe your cries
When you just wanted me, your home

And so, my dear, our first few months
Were coloured by these contrasts:
There was nothing more beautiful than our bond,
Yet I craved some time apart
And nothing was more bitter-sweet
Than the way that my touch soothed your cries
For like magic, it answered your every need,
Yet my own were left unsatisfied

I wept as I held you, and asked myself,
"What happened to my life?"
I had lost freedoms so small, I felt
I'd been robbed of my basic rights
For this bond of ours had become so strong
It had forged around me like chains,
And there we were tethered, for weeks on end
While I desperately wished things could change

My darling, as you've grown older -
It's very hard to describe -
The chains have loosened, you depend on me less,
So why does that make me cry?
I hold you, knowing that when you're placed
Into your cot, you'll stay -
My freedom reclaimed, yet I grieve the days
When only my arms made you feel safe

And this is it: the push and the pull
The feelings that roll like a tide
The desperate quest to find myself,
Yet the longing for you by my side
"It will get better as they grow,
They'll learn to settle apart"
And the words came true, yet I didn't expect
Their outcome would break my heart

The Early Days

And I know that it really doesn't make sense
That I wished you could sleep alone,
And yet now that you can, I mourn the days
When I was still your home
So now, whenever you need me again,
I'll hold you a little longer
And I'll relive the months that made
Our bond grow so much stronger

For Motherhood, it seems is full
Of these strange contradictions;
The things I wished away, now sweet
Nostalgia-fuelled addictions
And when our seasons change, and bring
long nights and stormy weather,
I'll hold you close, for seasons pass -
And so will these sweet days together.

Spring Rivers

I have felt the weight of the world:
A little over three kilograms
Like the moon's pull
It dragged me from my rest,
And as I held it, it seemed as though
The stars were all snuffed out
One by one
Until the night fell dark and empty

And I have known a brand-new sun
Bursting from my heart like galaxies
A million lights that
Reached the deepest trenches,
Thawing cold parts of me until
Love rushed through my veins
Like spring rivers,
Sweet and pure

It will make you old and young again
It will shift the axis of your earth
So that your very world spins differently

And you'll hear them call it
'A love like no other'
For it is the universe,
Held in your arms.

To Me, the Newborn Mother

The Early Days

It's blurry, but I remember,
I can see you standing there -
Your hands placed heavy on the sink,
Damp skin and dripping hair

You'd chanced a fleeting shower,
It was meant to be a "break"
Where blood mingled with phantom cries
Both dripping down the grate

And there you lingered, clinging
To the slipping solitude,
Knowing your baby waited for you -
A relentless cycle, renewed

And I still feel the swollen ache,
Skin fraying at the seams
Morning and night you patched yourself
With pads and balms and creams

While deeper was a different wound,
The kind that cannot be seen,
Since the birth it slowly leaked
The person you'd once been

What would I tell you, if I could?
Would I promise you that you'd heal?
That one day you'd recover
From this anguish that you feel?

For I still hear your voice shake,
Asking, "What am I doing wrong?
What happened to the life I knew?
When can I stop being strong?

"What if I'm not ready to be
The mother who must come last?
With needs, prioritised for months,
Now constantly surpassed?"

And on one of the darkest nights,
A question that made your heart break:
"Were we right to have this child?
Have we made an awful mistake?"

If only I could reach you
Through the heavy folds of time,
Hold your body in my arms,
As you shook with hopeless cries

Would there be anything I could say
That you hadn't heard before?
"This too shall pass", and something about
Long days, but years being short?

Yet we both know in those early weeks
Such sayings lose effect;
Like sunlight growing feeble
In the ocean's darkest depths

The Early Days

The fact is, I can't speak to you,
But perhaps, if you could hear,
I'd describe a truth in front of you
That's been blurred by your tears:

See their perfect sleeping form?
Their blissful angel's face?
The peace you see is all because
YOU made them feel so safe

See the way they gaze at you,
Love and trust in their eyes?
That look was forged in all the times
You answered their needs and cries

And soon you'll witness their first smile,
Do you know how they worked it out?
They mirrored you, when you smiled through
The tears, fatigue and doubt

I know your rage and frustration
Burn fiercely in those days,
But kindling that burns quickly
Soon, like ash, will drift away

And when you least expect it,
Your soul will begin to shake
And from that tremor, love will burst
With an earth-shattering quake

You'll press them close, lips in their hair,
Tears falling on their cheek,
And right there will be the answer to
That question you could hardly speak:

Mourn the old, for that life is gone,
But this new one was not a mistake;
For they are your homeland, heart and crown,
And the best decision you'll make

And I know you've heard all the clichés,
So I'll finish with something frank:
For all the things you love most about them,
It's YOU who deserves the thanks

So hear me when I tell you this,
For I assure you, it's the truth:

You should be so, so proud
This WILL get easier
Wounds do heal,

And you will be the proof.

The Early Days

Nightcall

It's a heavy dragging feeling
Hot eyes, foggy head
A weary ache around your neck,
The bedtime battle won.
You lift them into bed before
Sinking into your own,
Body fading into the mattress
Anchored by exhaustion

Close your eyes now,
Shutting them almost stings.
Limbs of lead, your mind already fading
As half-dreams drift between
Memories of the day
Relax your jaw
Shoulders sinking slowly

And just
As warm sleep
Blissfully enfolds you,
There comes a cry -
Short, high-pitched, piercing the night
The sound of heartbreak for you both
Your stomach drops cold
As you jerk awake,
Waiting,
But the cry continues.

Rub your face and
Wander in the dark to their side
Throat dry, brow knotted, eyes squinting.
A mumbled reassurance.
You reach to touch their chest
And two tiny hands hold on tight as you
Hum to them, deep and gentle.
Your song carrying through the dark.

You know it won't always be this way,
Coming and going in stages
As they need you less and less.
For now, you stay awake so that they may sleep
Your own bed growing cold.
Their steady sentinel in the dark
Abandoning rest to bring them peace.

The Early Days

The Spectre

If ever I have a moment,
A minute,
An hour, all to myself,
The seconds seem to pass differently

The absence of my baby
Seems to alter time's viscosity
And instead of moving through the hourglass
Like sand, smooth and steady,
Time rushes from me,
My solitude seeping like water
Through the cracks in my hands
Where I cupped it so desperately

And rather than feeling lighter,
My chest drags with the tug of
Impending responsibility

And rather than enjoying every second,
My mind calculates how many I have l left
Before you and I are together again -
The continuing cycle of inevitability

For my time was once my own, infinitely -
Yet when you arrived it became
A rare commodity

Please, do not misunderstand me:
For as soon as we are reunited,
The dragging feeling leaves me
And my heart sings just to
Set eyes on you once more

Yet, from the corner of my eye, I still see it -
It is the spectre of my own independence
Drifting from me again,
Just beyond my reach

Like a child's lost balloon, my time alone
Was a momentary novelty -
One that, for now,
I cannot keep.

Matrescence

Sun, Moon and Stars

They say that a mother's
Whole world is her children.
But do not forget -
If they are your world,
Then you are their moon,
You calm the rise and fall of their tides
You are their sun,
They thrive because your warmth gives them life
And you are all of their stars -
For stars shine on and on,
Across a universe of years
So that even their
Darkest nights may be
Filled with light.

The Pendulum

There will be days
When they will go down easily
And while they sleep,
A tune will hum happily from your lips
You'll cross items from a To-Do list
Sip a coffee and think,
"Maybe I can do this"
And there will be days
When you'll bury your face in a pillow
A scream will erupt from below,
Only to be muffled by
The strangle of week-old bedclothes
And you will sob and think,
"I cannot do this"
You will swing between this
Pendulum of emotional poles
Until they blur into
One experience:
The lightest highs and darkest lows
Of your matrescence.

Baby's Poem

Please stay with me, Mum-Mum,
I woke up with a pain
I need your help to soothe me, til I'm
Back to sleep again
Please just hold me, Mum-Mum,
It's warm here in your arms,
My cot was cold and I was scared
But here, I'm safe from harm

Please keep rocking, Mum-Mum
I know you work so hard,
Your list of jobs seems endless -
The kitchen, the washing, the yard,
Please wait with me, Mum-Mum
I know you've lots to do,
And once again it's all on hold
So that I can be with you

Please, no tears, my Mum-Mum,
I hate it when you weep,
I'm sorry I got upset again
Right when I was almost asleep,
Please cheer up, my Mum-Mum
I'm confused and overwhelmed,
And though it might not seem it,
It feels better just to be held

Matrescence

Please don't worry, Mum-Mum -
I need you so much now,
But one day I'll be as strong as you,
Because you showed me how,
And don't think too much, Mum-Mum,
Or wonder if I've regressed -
I'm learning that you'll always care,
If I'm hurt, upset or stressed

So please keep patting, Mum-Mum
My body's growing steady
I breathed your warm familiar scent,
And now my eyes are heavy
Keep on singing, Mum-Mum,
I'll remember every word
Your soft and gentle lullaby
Is the sweetest thing I've heard

I'm sleepy now, my Mum-mum
I know it took a while,
But it meant that as I closed my eyes
The last thing I saw was your smile.

Evening Prayer

Light fades
Clouds sink to the horizon,
A reef of indigo against a waning sky
Time turns ever closer to that hour
And the familiar feeling returns

Tonight, I grant myself the courage
To face the evening.
The patience to be there,
By your side
I remind myself to breathe,
To let my hands and arms and neck be soft
Despite the cries and chaos.
I surrender,
And to surrender means peace,
Not weakness.

I cannot make you go to sleep.

I can create the conditions
I can try to read your signs
I can sing, rock, pat and sway,
Though I can't control the outcome.
I can try to soothe your cries
And swallow my own
As we brave this storm together

For it is not my task to force you.
It is my role to support you.

Matrescence

And it's hard,
But you're not trying to make trouble -
You're just having trouble -
And I will be brave for you.

Though this road is rocky,
it will lead to rest for both of us.

This will not go on forever.
Eventually, you will sleep.

Night has fallen
Stars watch
From an infinite ink-dark sky
But I won't see them.

I'm here with you,
Your constant in the darkest hour
Your base, your home

So I grant myself the strength to breathe
And be your calm
Until you find your own.

Dear Old Me

Dear old me, I see you,
Before you were a mother,
Before you gave away one life
To care for the life of another

Dear old me, I see you,
How you seemed so free and young;
There was a lightness to you,
As if life had just begun

Dear old me, I see the way
You chose to spend your time;
You rested when you needed to,
To yourself, you were kind

How easily you satisfied
Your basic needs and cares -
For you possessed a freedom then
Of which you were hardly aware

You could do it all - or do nothing -
You showered and bathroomed at will,
Led days with spontaneity,
Or stayed in bed if ill

You left the house with little,
For you shouldered burdens few;
And most responsibilities
Began and ended with you

Matrescence

And even when you were upset,
(For life still had its sorrows),
You felt it at the forefront of
A time you need not borrow

Dear old me, I look back at you
And it hurts my heart to say
That you had no idea of what
Was soon coming your way

For as you grew that babe within,
Your hopes and joys grew, too,
How could you predict then, that soon,
Those joys would feel so few

For I see you, just weeks later,
You were bleeding from your breast,
Biting down on wooden spoons,
Tears landing on your chest

Oh, dear old me, you cried and begged
To be rid of that foul ache
And a tiny voice in you wondered
If you'd made a grave mistake

You were at rock bottom, then,
And couldn't see an end;
You were in too deep to see that, soon,
Both mind and body would mend

But the girl within the mirror then
Seemed so pale and disturbed,
You avoided her gaze, turning away
With a shrinking sense of worth

For how could you possibly be that girl
Who had been so free and sure?
You mourned the life that you had led,
For clearly, that life was no more

And you actually then began to believe
That the girl you'd been before
Must have died during the birth,
Bled out on the hospital floor

That she had somehow leaked from you,
Had spilled out from a wound
That must have formed within your soul
When your baby left the womb

That they had mopped up your old self
And cast you in the furnace;
Never to leave that birthing suite,
Never to resurface

Oh, dear old me, you didn't know yet
That your journey had just begun -
You didn't know that you'd look back
With pride at how far you've come

Matrescence

You didn't know that the girl you'd been
Had never really died -
True, she'd changed forever,
Yet not diminished, but amplified

You didn't know that, though it hurt
To shed your past existence,
It would forge such strength in you,
And newfound perseverance

And those little freedoms that you'd missed,
That you thought you'd never recover,
Inch by inch, minute by minute,
Soon you would rediscover

And dear old me, there'll be a force,
A healing you couldn't predict;
The sweetest spell around your soul,
Leaving your heart transfixed

The kind of love that floods your chest
And threatens to burst forth,
The kind of love that redefines
Your heart's sense of true north

That holds your hand, mends your wounds,
Shines purpose on your worth
With a light that surely, could only come
From an angel being here on Earth

No, it's true, you are no longer
That girl you were before…
It seems it was your destiny
To become their whole world.

And if it should still feel at times
That old life, you're still grieving,
Do shed those tears, my dear,
For tears are Nature's form of healing

And to that girl - I still miss you -
But I can truly vow
That there is nothing I would trade
For the woman, the mother
I am now.

Matrescence

Call You Mine

Let my clothes be stained
And hair look plain
Adorne me with smears of chalk
And grubby finger-painting

Let the shadows settle and lie
Deep beneath my eyes,
Let my face be bare, and body soft
In the places where it nurtured you

Let my arms grow strong with that
Sacred muscle memory of
All the times I lifted you -
Because one day, my muscles will forget.

And let my skin wrinkle,
Every line is a symbol of
The way you made me smile

For I know that these years
Are a fraction of your future,
But in my heart, you're my whole lifetime -

So rather than perfection
Let me wear the signs
That once, I was lucky enough
To call you mine.

On Air

Imagine if all mothers
Had a switch by them at night,
And a board fitted with a thousand little lights,
So that when they are awake
And feeling lost and lonely in the long dark,
They could press their little switch -
As if to say, "On Air" -
And in response, the board would ignite
With the glow of a hundred lights the same
Of other mothers who've turned their switches on,
Awake, feeding, soothing
At that very moment.
And in the night the room would be lit with the glimmer
Of an alliance of stars,
Saying, "You may be on your own,
But you are not alone".

Coexist

Once, satisfaction was as simple as
Writing a To-Do list
Working through it steadily
A careful line through each completed task

Once, freedom felt like
Replying with calm fingers
A moment taken for careful thought
And fixing typos didn't feel a luxury

Once, self care was
Hearing my body cry for rest
And answering it, for the time was my own
And I could spend it all on me

Now we're stuck in limbo
Time suspended in a
Mess of scattered toys and dust
The same nursery rhymes skipping on repeat

And rather than written on paper,
The tasks weigh down around my head,
Pressing on my shoulders,
Suffocating in their silent demand

And I love you, I love being your mother
But beneath that love
Is a yearning for a time that was
In itself, my own

Back then, I knew 'busy'.
I knew long hours, unpaid overtime
More tasks than time, but at least the only
Responsibilities were mine

I've held a leaky bladder just to
Let you sleep a little longer
I've gazed at a water bottle only
Slightly out of reach

For it's not the wild nights I miss,
It's the minute freedoms,
Before my needs were
Eternally demoted

And though I've known no greater joy
Than your perfect little smile
Your rolly-polley arms and
Your happy cackle

And though I know one day
This nest will be empty
And I'll ache to put anything on hold
To have you in my home, my arms

For now, I still dream of freedom,
For these feelings can coexist.

Golden Honey

And if you ask me
What I remember from those early years,
I will picture that single curl
Where it rested against the
Sweet little nape of your neck,
The way I'd gaze at it when you played
With your back toward me.
I'll wrap my old arms around me
And remember the weight
Of your tired little body,
And the soft face that rested on my chest
And I hope beyond hope that
I'll always remember the way that the bathwater
Made petals of your eyelashes,
Framing those delicate daisy-eyes,
So that the image might be preserved
Like pressed flowers
Between pages of my memory

And if you ever ask me
To tell you a story from when you were young,
I know I won't think of the dark days.
I know I won't think of the ways that
I sometimes felt I was breaking,
The days that I barely made it through,
For those memories are cold and brief
And even Winter's hardest frosts can thaw.
So I'll tell you about
How you were the sun -
How you were morning light, clear and bright
How you were rosy cheeks
Sunflower smiles, warm and funny,
Golden-honey joy
I'll tell you about how your little heart
Loved so easily, it overflowed -
Spilled sweetly into the cracks in my soul
Diffused my doubts and soothed fears
Made me laugh again, even through tears.

And it will sound like just another family story
The time you made Mum laugh
Because you did that something silly,
Told so many times, it makes you roll your eyes -

But I will smile and know
Those are the stories
Of how your love made me whole.

Full Circle

You slept in my arms and I daydreamed
About a time when you had grown
When the halcyon days of 'just us' had passed
And I wasn't all you'd known

You went to school, ran from the car
Without a second word
Came home with tales of brand-new friends
And everything you'd learned

You spoke of your teacher with wonder and awe
(They did sound fantastic to me)
And beneath the pride that filled my heart
Was a twinge of jealousy

You slept in my arms and I daydreamed
This time you were bigger again
The friends we had known had been replaced
And so much of you had changed

For now when I asked, "How was school?"
You'd simply reply, "It was fine."
And there was something between us
A distance, an unspoken line

And you and I would have terrible fights
As teens and parents do,
Your words like wounds on a heart that once
Was all that mattered to you

And so for those years I watched from the side
I no longer knew your heart
Still part of your life, not the middle,
Together, but somehow apart

You slept in my arms and I daydreamed
You were finding your way through life
You studied or worked, lived with friends
Or maybe a husband or wife

You dreamed of a future you wanted,
How to get there you still didn't know
We'd listen in quiet disbelief
At how much our baby had grown

Or maybe (I shuddered at the thought)
Life would deal you pain
Your heart broken by someone else
Then mended, then broken again

And as I imagined you grieving
It broke my own heart too
Because, to me, our hearts were one
The bond between me and you

You slept in my arms and I daydreamed
You'd had a babe of your own
A brand-new life, filling yours
With a love you'd never known

Matrescence

We sat together like old friends do
Watching their sleeping form,
I was content, yet wondered still
Where those decades had gone

For we had come full circle
You an adult, me growing old
You'd learned the way a child could
Divide you at your soul

For part of you lived within them now
You said, "It's strange, you know,
I've sat and wondered who they'll be,
Yet I'm scared to watch them grow"

And I felt my voice was breaking
As I reached to take your hand,
I smiled as I wept, and whispered,
"Yes, I understand."

Love Her Like You

Days are growing long again,
The evenings staying warm
And in my mind an old concern
Appears to have reformed

This body of mine has changed
Since it brought you to my side,
I see her in the mirror and
Quickly avert my eyes

Clothes and swimwear worn before
Would never fit me now;
I hold them up in front of me
And simply wonder, "how?"

And I can feel this body shake
As I carry you around
Parts that once were smooth and lean
Now moving, soft and round

So I wonder, am I brave enough
To strip off and be bare?
Will they think, "Gosh, she has let go",
Or simply stop and stare?

I wonder, am I bold enough
To play with you by the sea?
Without my hands drifting to cover
Those awkward parts of me?

Matrescence

And I can try to tell myself
That it's all in my head
That they'd be busy watching
The cute baby play, instead

But a little part of me still mourns
The body I once knew
For somehow, I feel less bold now,
Since growing and birthing you

And suddenly it hits me:
The sadness of it all –
That creating you, perfection, made
My own self-worth feel small

My pregnant form drew compliments,
They said that I was glowing
And now I hide the evidence,
I pray it isn't showing

And I realise it's ironic:
I did something so, so brave,
It left a mark on me that now, just
Makes me feel ashamed

Yet this body of mine made magic
When it sheltered you inside
It stretched and grew, protected you
'Til I roared you to my side

I took my blood and made it yours
Crafted your little heart,
Then made it beat, with nothing more
Than Mother Nature's spark

And then I leaked a milk that was alive
And tailor-made for you
I struggled through the pain, nurtured you
On the outside, too

Yes, I went through something that
Only mothers truly know
It transformed me inside and out,
So why shouldn't it show?

And if people see the difference
Well, that won't matter now
I'll find the beauty in my body
And you will show me how

For when you look at me, my dear
You see your favourite things:
The arms you love to rest between,
The lips that kisses bring

You look at me as though I am
The goddess of all mothers
You love me as I am right now,
You wouldn't have any others

Matrescence

So I'll take off my clothes and
Feel the sun warming my skin
The sun and I, we've both made life
And I'm letting warmth back in

I'll take your little hand,
And hold your body against mine
I'll be proud of what my body did:
It made something divine

And once we're home, and you're to bed,
My reflection will come into view
I'll try to see that girl the same
Way that you see her, too

For the veins, the dimples and the curves,
The bits I've tried to hide,
If I never had them, I'd never have you,
The angel by my side

And if I feel unsure again
In this new skin of mine
I'll try to love her like you do,
Even one little bit at a time.

Some Days

Some days, we sit motionless
Surrounded by chaos, an island of idleness
In a sea of neglected responsibility,
While all the things that I need to do
Watch from their tall towers,
Waiting where they have been allowed to pile up -
My To-Do list, spread from my overflowing head
Destined to be forgotten amongst the
Scattered clothes, dirty dishes
Discarded toys and too much screen time.
You rest in my arms, the only place that brings you peace,
While my unproductivity itches at me
Until I realise that even my body feels grubby,
The sweat and grime just another sign
That everything else comes second -
And, it feels, at very bottom of that list,
Is me.

These are the hardest days, I whisper to myself.
The long labours. The weary years.
And though it's another challenge, it's ultimately kinder
To give myself the reminder that
Some day, things will not be this way.
For now, the rest can wait.
So I make the decision
To block the mess from my peripheral vision
And gaze at the achievement I make every single day:
The one that I hold in my arms -
You.

If It Weren't for You

If it weren't for you,
I'd have finished that weeks ago.
If it weren't for you,
I'd never have had to rush.
And at the end of a busy day,
Once things were neatly put away,
I'd have looked forward to bed -
For bed would have meant rest,
If it weren't for you

If it weren't for you,
I wouldn't have missed that appointment
Forgotten that bill and let that thing run out
And if it weren't for you,
I'd have been more clear -
I wouldn't have gotten so muddled -
Because sometimes I struggle to
Even make sense anymore
And my mind wouldn't be so heavy
If it weren't for the weight of you.

And if it weren't for you,
My body wouldn't wear the signs
In the places where it carried you before,
And it wouldn't ache
In the places where I carry you with me now
And I wouldn't have to wake,
Haunting this house like a ghost,
Drifting towards the sound of your cries
Treading a path so familiar
It could be mirrored
In the map of my veins

And if it weren't for you,
Perhaps I wouldn't have snapped
Lost my temper somewhere in the debris
Of this chaotic normality
And the rage might not have risen
Like fork-tongued flames
Licking up through my chest,
Roaring out from my mouth,
Reducing the room to ash
And afterward, leaving us to
Sit alone
In the quiet
And the dust

And yet,
If weren't for you,

Matrescence

I wouldn't have known the strength of these bones
Heard the Earth's power erupt from my lungs
And felt an ancestry of Mothers watching over me
As I sounded your entrance into the world
And if it weren't for you,
I wouldn't have known that
Angels lived on here on Earth -
For I saw one in
The moment you arrived

And if it weren't for you,
I'd never have known that
My heart could leave my breast
And live within another's,
For it passed through my skin and into yours
As soon as you were placed upon my chest

And if it weren't for you,
I'd never have felt my breath catch as I
Stroked your perfect skin,
Brushed my lips through your silky hair
Held you, cradled you in your
Perfect vulnerability,
Your heaven-sent fragility,
And all at once felt the storm of responsibility
As I realised that your safety depends on me,
And I'd never have known that
Your birth formed an ancient pact,
A binding contract that
Imprinted your soul on mine
Forevermore

MUSE

My child, if it weren't for you,
I don't think I would ever understand
Or have felt prepared
To do anything,
Anything,
To protect the life of another
For becoming a Mother makes me willing to
Give   my   life
To guarantee yours

For the very turn of the earth
P a u s e s
When your little eyes shine into mine

And when you sleep, the beat of time
S l o w s
As I gaze upon your face,
Serene and still
In the warmth of our embrace

And I know now
That I would never have a love
This fierce and tender,
This agonising and healing,
Soul-crushing, and yet life-giving,

If it weren't for you.

Matrescence

The Moon and the Tide

Early, the sickness came in waves
It swelled in me like a tide
And in waves my body surged until
You finally arrived

And after, I seemed to float with ease
Just off a sun-drenched shore
The water warm, my feet steady
Where they touched the ocean floor

Yet I soon began to crash and dump
On jagged rocks and sand
Then retreated, rushing, snatched by a rip
That dragged me far from land

Out there the sea was black and cold
And the undertow was fierce
Tumbling in currents beneath the depths
Of a surface I could not pierce

The sun still shone, but from down there
It was distant, weak and pale
And I was sinking, drowning in
The pain, the fear, the fails

So I drifted far - but when I woke
My dear, soon I had found
You'd rescued me, and once again
I stood on solid ground

Because even when a storm hits,
You're the moon, and I'm the tide
I thought I had to lead, but
It was you who was my guide

Your bright eyes were my lighthouse
Brought me back from darkest dark
And your smile was a tonic for
My weary, aching heart

For I had shed so many tears
It formed a tidal wave
And though it swept me far from home,
In the end, it made me brave

So when waves come, we'll sail
From the storm into the sun
Transporting us from who we were,
To who we will become

Matrescence

And we'll navigate together
This new land we've come upon
Perhaps we'll feel at home here
Even when the sun has gone

For the moon brings light to this world
With an iridescent shimmer
And the tide reflects the moon
And it's pure and gentle glimmer

So that even in the darkness
Our hearts will surely glow,
And like the tide, there's beauty here
With every ebb and flow.

Growing

We are both still growing
You, brand new from seed -
Your limbs, so soft, like sweet young stems,
Seem longer with each feed
And we are both still learning;
I've weathered wind and rain,
My branches battered months on end,
Splintering in pain.

It's Spring, yet we're still changing,
We reach to a brand new sun -
Its light a little different
Since the day you came along,
And now we are both blooming
Each day our roots grow long,
And as they near each other,
They're entwining, twice as strong.

I Go to You

Washing baskets overflow behind a
Highchair that still needs cleaning,
Toys lay littered among gathering dust,
And the inbox in my mind
Screams for a response.
But you need me again,
So I go to you.
One day,
The washing will be neatly away
The highchair sold
The toys long outgrown and the dust wiped away
An empty house,
A quiet phone
And the only message I'll be craving will be yours -
Because you won't always need me this way .
One day,
You might not
Need me at all.

So now, I go to you.

Paradox

I could hold you here forever
And I crave some time alone
I love to watch you changing
And I wish you wouldn't grow
I count the hours 'til bedtime
And I miss you when you sleep
I've never known such happiness,
And still I ache and weep
And sometimes, I've felt broken
I never knew I could be this strong
I've had nothing in me left to give,
Yet still, I carried on
I've dreamt of something different
I wouldn't change this for the world
I've stepped across the threshold now,
And still, I'm that same girl
I dread the day I can't keep you safe
Yet one day, I must let go -
I'll lay awake, wondering where time went
While I wait for you to come home
For you are my heaviest burden
And my sweetest, purest light -
My life has never felt this hard
And never shone so bright
And though it is a paradox,
One thought does not cancel the other;
For these are the truths that both exist
Within the heart of a mother.

Do Not Tell Me

Do not tell me that
Women are the weaker sex
When we have used nothing but
The cells in our blood and the
Beating of our hearts to grow
The entirety of humanity
When we have reached down
Inside ourselves,
Scrambling, clutching desperately
At every ounce of strength
And spark of energy
So that we could push and roar 'til we
Bled all over the floor -
When we have fought a mental battle
As we are cut open,
Straight through our middle,
Hands pulling at our insides
Just to bring their
Little bodies into the light

And do not tell me that
Mothers are not strong, when,
Newly stitched together,
Still bleeding,
Still reeling from the trauma,
We have reduced the priority
Of our own recovery
Held a screaming babe to our
Cracked and oozing nipples
Grit our teeth and found
Something to bite down on
As we face the excruciating price of
Nurturing our young:
The pain was not over
With the birth -
The next ordeal has just begun

Matrescence

And do not shame us
If we do not choose the breast.
How could you possibly understand
What that mother needs best?
For she has worked just as hard -
You do not see her awake in the dark,
Kettle-boiling, sterilising,
Calculating and preparing,
Measuring powders in those
Long and lonely hours,
Or attached to a machine,
To pump or store, pump and store,
For weeks or months or more.
Her decisions have a validity
Far greater than your commentary.
For where others may breastfeed,
She nurtures her babe just as dearly.

And so, please
Do not have the audacity
Or try to take the liberty
To tell us when, where, or how we
Should feed our babies.
You would worship our nipples with
Feverish sexuality
Until you witness them used
For their sacred purpose,
And suddenly they are
Disgusting, inappropriate, perverse.
And even some would
Lust after our breasts, and
In the same breath
Shame mothers for not using them
(Yet, when we do,
You do not want to see them)
And then, when they grow soft
And sag from feeding,
Would laugh and suggest
That surgery is needed.

Matrescence

If you have not
Been where we have gone,
Do not tell us
Where our journey should
Begin or end -
For some of us have
Been to hell and back in our effort
To make their world heaven.
And do not tell us
That the world's idea of 'power'
Refers to faceless figures
Way up in high towers.
Who could be stronger
Than those who have loved this fiercely
Through their darkest, hardest hours?
Who wake up and brave the day,
No matter what it brings,
To find their greatest joy in
Smiling down at those
Wide eyes and milky grins.

Grief, Life and Loss

Grief, Life and Loss

Our Friend Up In The Stars

My Baby,
There's someone very dear to me
Who I long for you to know
You didn't get a chance to meet
Before they had to go
And since you came into my life
I'm finding, more and more,
Their absence feels much greater
Than it ever did before

You're changing, growing, learning skills,
We're so amazed by you,
But as I clap and laugh and cheer
I wish they could see you, too
For I know that they'd be terribly proud
Of us, of how hard we've tried -
If they were here, my dear, you'd be
The greatest joy in their life

This person once lived here on Earth
The same as you and I,
Now you'll find them in a sunrise,
In the stars, the sea, the sky
And if you listen to the trees
When a breeze drifts along,
You might just hear them hum to you
Their soft and gentle song

So tell me, did you know them
When you lived among the stars?
Were they your friend up there before
You came down to my arms?
Did they sing to you, hold you,
Teach you things,
And tell you about their life,
Then release you gently, to part as friends
When it was finally your time?

For even though my heart aches
That they never knew your name,
I know that part of them still runs
Within your perfect veins
And though that gap feels empty
Since they drifted far above,
It seems the wound is healing
With this new and tender love

So we'll sit close, my darling
On a warm and starry night
I'll tell you of this person
Who once made my life so bright
We'll speak of them as though perhaps,
They aren't so very far,
For you would have been adored by them,
Our friend up in the stars.

No More Will We Feed

I guess I knew our time would come,
Though I didn't think so soon;
I thought that I'd be feeding you
Beneath many coming moons

You've grown into a big girl, now -
Overnight, it seems -
You've decided you no longer need
Our special, sacred feeds

And now, rather than seeking it,
You tell your Mumma, "No!"
I laugh, and say, "Okay!",
Blinking back the tears that flow

So no more will we feed, my dear,
Your tummy close to mine,
No, you won't gaze up at me,
Blinking with sweet owl's eyes

Never again will nursing you
Instantly soothe your cries,
Never again will your body
Be nurtured straight from mine

And I know that I once hated it;
I howled, and told your Gran
When you were only two weeks old
That I'd never feed you again

And I know that we were so lucky
To be able to feed at all;
I know if we'd taken a different path,
Things would still have been as special

But perhaps that's why I'm grieving so,
For we fought to make this work;
Just thinking of our gruelling start
Is what makes this ending hurt

And so I'll smile, rather than weep;
I just wish I'd been aware
That our last feed was indeed the last
That we would ever share

It's not just that we've stopped, my dear,
It's what it represents:
You're growing up, and though that's grand,
You'll need me less and less

And that is the way that motherhood goes,
In the chaos, we carry on,
Not noticing as days pass us by,
Until they are already gone

Yet I know those precious months
Have bound us, deep and sure;
I hope, though we won't feed again,
We'll be close forevermore

And though I'm feeling sad for now,
I know that, from your birth,
Our time won't just be marked by 'lasts',
But beautiful, heart-warming 'firsts'.

Back to the Rocking Chair

When I am old, I will close my eyes
And place my hands on my womb
I'll remember the songs that I whispered then,
Back when it was filled with you

For you were there, you heard me,
And from then I was never alone
But only I will remember those months
When I was your very first home

And when I am old, I will close my eyes
And remember a time that has passed
Only my heart can ever recall
Our hours alone in the dark

Though you were there, you'll never know
How it felt to hold you close,
How to kiss your sleeping angel's-eyes
Made a lump form in my throat

And when I am old I'll recall the way
That you huddled against my chest
A chubby hand as soft as silk
Absently tracing my breast

For nobody else in the world but me
Will remember you quite that way,
How I'd measure your fingers against my own
Wishing so small, they would stay

And one day when I am old as old,
And it's time for me to go,
I know those memories will light the dark
With a warm, familiar glow

I wonder, might you hold my hand
When I finally leave this place?
So I may gaze upon you just once more,
And remember my baby's face?

And our roles, they will have shifted then,
So that baby looks down on mother
Stroking my forehead to soothe a pain
From which we know I'll never recover

Weep not, my babe, for I won't be scared
When life lays me at that door
Because I'll be returning to
A place I knew before

Yes, when I am very old, please know
That when I leave this place behind,
I'll be going back to those memories
I'll have treasured in my mind

For I am sure in my heart now
That whenever I finally leave,
I'll going back to the rocking chair
When it was just you and me

And I'll be young once more, my babe,
And you'll be tiny again
And we'll cuddle for eternity,
Right where it all began

For that must be why the memories
Can only ever be mine,
It's so that I can rest right there
And stay for all of time

And from there we'll watch you peacefully,
Living on with your family,
For I'll be with you again, my dear
In those sacred memories

Your silky hair upon my arm,
Little body against my own,
The rocking chair, just you and me -
Will be our forever home.

The Angels

Once, there was a star above
Whose light shone down on Earth
Where a longing family waited
For this sweet new baby's birth

Yet on its journey to this world,
Their star began to change;
It once shone bright, so full of life,
But now, that light had waned

A family waited with bated breath
For the baby they'd longed to meet,
Yet before their child reached their arms,
Its sweet heart ceased to beat

And so, this family found themselves
With empty hands and souls
Grieving for a babe who, now,
They'd never get to know

Their hearts yearned for a future
Which, it seemed, life would not bring;
For their little babe had drifted back
Beneath Mother Nature's wings

"What was it that we did wrong?"
They cried as they held each other,
"Why did we have to farewell our babe,
While others reach their mothers?"

As time passed, this mother learned
She had done no wrong at all,
Yet in quiet moments, she wondered still
Why Nature had made this call

For this mother was left with a gap in her heart
The size and shape of her babe,
And as time passed, she would dream
Of that child that she had craved

Sometimes, often late at night,
She wonders where they are;
Perhaps they sleep in the softest of clouds,
Nestled between heaven's stars

And even though her heart still aches
To hold her babe in her arms,
She knows that now, they rest in peace,
Eternally safe from harm

She knows that they are never alone,
For they rest with many others:
The angel-babes who stayed up above,
Never forgotten by their mothers

"A baby, now and forever," she thinks,
"A babe who will always be mine;
Sleep steady in your slumber,
In my heart, for all of time".

In Every Lifetime

If I had never had you,
If I'd never been a mother,
I wonder if somehow we would have
Still found each other -
Two strangers drawn together
By some divine encounter
For when I hold you to my chest
And calm your tearful shudders,
I can't help but believe our souls
Were meant for one another.
Perhaps, in every lifetime,
You're my babe, and I'm your mother,
Maybe in every universe
Fate brings our hearts together
For if it's true, then when I'm old
And have lived my final summer,
There'll be comfort in knowing
Wherever I go,
You and I will find each other.

'Til The End

To my little one,

I think it was the Greeks who said
The Fates controlled our lives,
They pulled the strings of destiny,
Chose how we'd live, and die

And I've been blessed, my dear,
Since they entwined your life with mine -
Not sure if I believe in Gods
Yet I've witnessed the Divine

And they wove us such a love story,
It must have been foretold;
When you came into my life
My strings were spun from straw to gold

My little one, there is a truth
That I don't want to face -
One day, the Fates will break the string
That ties me to this place

It's not that I worry for myself,
For one day, we all must go,
Yet there's still so much to tell you,
Things I hope you'll always know

Grief, Life and Loss

And I don't know when I'll leave this world
But darling, before I do,
My only hope is to tell you
How much your Mummy loved you

So if I go tomorrow
If I suddenly leave this place
If I never get the chance
To tell you all this, face-to-face,

Just know that I have loved you
Since you landed on my chest,
Just know, of all the days I've lived,
The days of you have been my best

And it's hard to find the words,
But we're connected, of that I'm sure -
I think part of my heart and soul
Left me, just to form yours

So if I go tomorrow
If I'm wiped out by a bus
If I slip down some steep stairs
Or my brain suddenly goes bust

MUSE

Just know that when I watched you,
It was my heart that I was seeing -
I couldn't believe how my whole world
Could exist in one tiny being

And just so that you know,
We had a ball, you and I together,
Just so that you know,
I wished those days would last forever

For you are my muse, my everything
My sidekick, thick as thieves,
My best friend, my beloved,
The greatest thing I have achieved

You're my angel, my high-heaven,
The sweetest soul I've ever known
And every day I lived with you
I was blessed to be never alone

So if I go tomorrow
And we don't get to share our lives,
Know that my last days were full of joy
Just because you were alive

And know that I'll still be here
In those things that get passed on;
The photos of us, the lullabies
That I know you'll still be sung

For those are the sweetest moments
That I've loved the very best
Hours alone, just you and I
Our hearts pressed, chest-to-chest

And I hope you'll have these words now,
Though they capture only a glimpse
Of a love that defies life and death,
A love that cannot be eclipsed

So if I go tomorrow
If the Fates take my string with their sheers,
Never can they undo the bonds where
It was wound with yours for these years

And if words have any power,
I hope these words will help you to mend -
And just know that I loved you,
I loved you, I loved you,
'Til the end.

A Love That Was Like No Other

Sometimes, when we lose loved ones,
Reminders appear without warning -
An image, a sound, or something they loved,
And triggers the pain of mourning

And we find ourselves hurting all over again
When we thought we were just getting stronger
We find ourselves wishing we'd had more time,
That they could have stayed just a bit longer

And the old familiar pain returns,
The burning ache of grief
We understand - all life must end -
Yet we still feel that death is a thief

I don't know if the pain ever leaves us,
Its tides rise and fall with time
But maybe one day those reminders
Will no longer ache, but shine

And instead of pulling us downward,
These memories of love and joy
Will help to lift us up again -
Not longer anchors, but lifebuoys

And we'll see them again in a sunrise
In the stars, the sea, the sky
We'll hear them when the leaves move
As a gentle breeze goes by

And we'll close our eyes, wondering
About where they might be now,
Perhaps they are back in those golden days
And they're young again somehow

For they cannot ever leave us
If they stay in our memories,
And their life still runs through the very veins
Of their living legacies

And so we feel this pain together
Yet we comfort one another,
For we know that grief is the price we must pay
For a love that was like no other.

Friends and Lovers

Simple Privilege

We can talk about grand gestures
Yet it is a simple and
Precious privilege
To have a friend, who,

Even from beneath
Their own rain cloud,

Can still extend
Three words:

"How are you?"

Dear Mum

Dear Mum,
In the past, I've thanked you
"For all that you've done for me",
Yet recently I've come to learn
What those words truly mean

Something has changed within me, Mum,
I'm no longer that same girl
I've crossed over a threshold,
Stepped into another world

It seems the light is different here,
It's changed all I once knew,
And now I have come face-to-face
With another side of you

Some nights, I have been wide awake
Rocking my babe in the dark,
Thinking, is this how you held me, too?
With my head pressed against your heart?

Did you ever gaze at me and wish
That you could just pause time?
Or study my tiny features, and think
"How could you really be mine?"

Did you ever have the strangest sense
That I was still part of you?
That my soul extended from your own,
That my heart was your heart, too?

Friends and Lovers

And Mum, did you ever mourn the girl
That you had been before?
I'm nervous to say, but were there days
You just didn't want to be "Mum" anymore?

For this is what I've been through, Mum
And it's made me weep for you
Wondering if this is what
You went through for me, too

I know I have not journeyed far
Down this path of motherhood,
Yet the extent of what you've done for me
Is slowly being understood

So Mum, I deeply thank you
For those long and loving years
When you sacrificed it all and gave
Your strength, your heart, your tears

Thank you for shouldering broken sleep,
And soothing my little head,
Thank you for laying twisted and stiff
So that I could share your bed

Thank you for singing through the pain
As you nursed me at your breast
Thank you for rocking me, hours on end
In the arms that I loved best

And thanks for greeting me every day
With games and songs and smiles,
I hope the love and joy we've shared
Helped make it all worthwhile

I'm sorry for all the times we fought,
As do all girls and their mothers,
My words like barbs, piercing a heart
That had loved me like no other

And I really mean it when I say
It's a privilege, sure and true,
To navigate my motherhood
With a compass whose North is you

For life has come full-circle,
Now I nurse my own baby,
Whispering those lullabies
That you once sang to me

Friends and Lovers

So Mum-Mum, if you wondered then
As you held me, just us two,
Whether I'd ever understand
Those years of me and you

How it felt to put yourself second
So that I always came first,
Exhausted by a perfect love
That made your whole heart burst

It seems this baby has been a gift,
A mirror into our pasts,
Reflecting a time when I was your babe,
A time of firsts, and lasts

And though your efforts then are still
Being understood by me,
I've always carried those days with me -
For our love is their legacy

So thank you, Mum, for something
That in my heart I always knew:
I know who loved me like no one else could,
It was you, it was you, it was you.

In the Trenches

We're deep down in the trenches
My baby and I.
While she sleeps I work quickly,
Reinforcing the muddy sides
Patching the leaks
Digging out a place for her that's sheltered,
warm and safe
But there's dark water creeping in,
Pooling around our feet
And as I work my arms grow heavy
And something drags within my chest.

A friend walks by and peers down at us.
"How are you going?" she asks.
I call up to her: "we're good!"
But my voice is small and thin,
Echoing up the cliff sides
And I notice that the trench has become a ravine -
When did that happen?
The water is up to my knees.

"Just let me know if I can help," calls the friend.
I thank her, looking down at my baby
as she floats in the raft that I built her.
I haven't started on my own yet.
The friend is a distant silhouette up there
where the sun blazes.
She disappears.

Friends and Lovers

Night falls and the water grows cold
I shiver, holding the little raft above me as the
Dark water now laps around my neck
"Don't worry", I whisper to my babe.
"They say this is temporary."
But my feet can no longer touch the bottom
And we're only just treading water
And there's a current now,
Pulling me under.

Somehow, even as we're sinking in the dark
I can see my baby smiling at me
Wide eyes, still full of joy
And my heart aches for her innocence
And in the mirror of her eye, there's a sparkle
Growing bigger - it's shining now -
And I realise it's a reflection;
There's a light at the top of the ravine.
The friend has returned.

"I know you said you didn't need anything,"
She calls.
But she's lowering down a ladder
Throwing me a life ring
Reaching out her hand.
She's here.
And as we pull ourselves upwards to the safety
Of firm, dry earth,
I see the dawn.

To Our Shore

This ship of ours has weathered
Through rain and stormy seas,
Some days, the helm is steered by you,
And other days, by me

We've skirted swells and deep whirlpools
And perilous jagged reefs
And changing winds that swept us far
From where we planned to be

We've woken blindly, lost in mists
So stagnant, still and grey
That we could neither see ahead
Nor recall our recent days

But my love, this ship is solid,
For we built it on our own -
And though marked by our journey,
It still will guide us home

And the currents, they will settle
And the gales will gust no more,
And the sun will gently clear the mist
As we sail to our shore.

Note to My Love

My love,
I think we traded our youth for theirs,
Our sleep-ins for sleepless nights,
Spontaneous plans became Groundhog Day
Where exhaustion begins at first light

And dinner dates turned into bedtime routines,
'Til we wade through the ruins of the day,
Collapsing in bed, exhausted and spent
With hardly a word left to say

And when was the romance and ease eclipsed
By bickering and barked instructions?
It seems we lost all of our patience and care
In our constant struggle to function

Yet, here in the chaos, I watch you with them,
And there's pure magic in your smile
And there is a promise, right here and now,
That these years will all be worthwhile

For you glance at me, a single look,
Saying, "Can you believe what we made?"
And your eyes are wide with love and pride
As we gaze upon our babe
And yes, our freedoms are put on hold,
But my love, they'll be regained,
And we'll laugh and reminisce and know
It was all a worthy trade

And so my heart sings as I smile back,
Nodding, yet not a word spoken,
For in that moment we both know
Our love was never broken.

To My Darling

My Darling, do you remember
What we did before they were born?
When we spent our lives together,
And slept later than dawn

We knew no limits to our time,
No boundaries to our days
We whiled-away long afternoons
In peaceful sun-soaked haze

My Darling, do you remember
The moment it all changed?
Those two pink lines, your eyes met mine,
We'd never be the same

And though I carried them in me,
You carried us both with you -
You clutched my hand through tests and scans,
The nerves, the joy, yours too

And later on, you nurtured me
In the weeks when I was ill
My nurse, my maid, saviour and friend,
Every want or need, you filled

Tell me, do you remember
Those first kicks we could feel?
Your hand on me, our hearts alight
We knew then - this was real

And when it was finally time
You cradled me as I surged
You held me, soothed me, gave me strength
'Til they finally emerged

And Darling, I still hear your voice
As it broke, when you said to me:
"You did it", and we both wept then,
As our hearts soared to infinity

When I look back, and think of these years,
The memory I'll treasure most
Is watching you fall in love with them -
And the bond between you both

For I knew you had the power to love,
I knew your gentle soul,
But becoming a parent has surely been
Your most brave and tender role

My darling, I can see it
When you look into their eyes,
My darling, I can see it there -
The way they've changed your life

And I know we mourn those old selves now,
For since, it seems we've become
So tired, heavy, and short-tempered,
Aged years in the space of months

Friends and Lovers

I know it's hard living this way -
Like two ships that pass in the night -
Whispered arguments, broken sleep,
And days that begin before light

Yes, we have lost those afternoons,
Those selves who were so young,
Yet I would never trade them
For the person you've become

My love, this is why I need for you
To hear something from me:
This time is not forever,
These years are temporary

And though we know they will be hard,
And grind on us heavily,
They too will be the making of
Our fondest memories

One day, we'll curl up in bed,
Our bodies marked with age,
And we will laugh and weep to think
Of when they were just babes

"Remember when?" we'll whisper,
"Remember that trick they had?"
"Can you believe those years are gone,
When we were first Mum and Dad?"

And the lack of sleep, the bickering,
The having-no-idea-at-all,
And the long neglected intimacies
Won't be what we'll recall,

It will be the first smiles, the first few words,
The very first "I love you"
It will be the way they still fit in our arms,
In these years that are fleeting and few

And, my love, there's one more thing
I so terribly need to say,
It's about the things you do for us,
Each and every day

For I feel I rarely get the chance
To stop and recognise
The way you work so tirelessly for
This family and our lives

It doesn't go unnoticed,
Even if it seems ignored -
If only you knew what a saviour you are
When you come home through that door

And so, these words from my own heart
Will finish with just these two:
(My dear, my soul, my darling love,
Now and forever),
Thank you.

Poems from the Pandemic

In the Year that I Was Born

Dear Mumma,
One day, when I'm in History class
They'll talk about a year -
A year that plagued the whole wide world
With illness, change and fear

They'll show us on a map the way it
Spread here, to our home
How lockdowns kept us safe, and yet
Also kept us alone

We'll learn about the politics,
The vaccines and the science
We'll study graphs and charts
That measured test-result reliance

But there'll be something missing
From those busy textbook pages,
Something about that year that
Won't be studied through the ages

For Mumma, they won't know
That in that year, you were transformed
That your life was changed forever,
In the year that I was born

And while the world was mourning
Those freedoms they once knew,
You also mourned the girl you were,
For she was missing, too

And in her place was a mother,
Still in shock, so new to it all
So far from the family who wanted to help
From the other end of a call

Yet all the graphs and charts we see
Will not record the way
That you stayed home, alone with me
For day, after day, after day

The news reports will not discuss
How you learned to mother, alone
And the footage will not document
Those lonely weeks at home

And the quotes, they will not be from you
As you tearfully cried to me,
"My darling, I love you so much,
But this isn't how it should be"

And the speeches from our leaders,
So formal, rehearsed and long,
Will seem pale against the magic
Of our sacred bed-time songs

MUSE

For Mumna, you may have felt so lost
In the months we spent alone,
But you were all I needed,
You were all I'd ever known

And I know you'll probably wonder
If I'll ever understand,
How hard it was to find yourself
With so few helping hands

But please, Mumma, know this now:
Those months, they formed a bond,
A closeness that will stay with us
For years and decades long

It formed when you were rocking me,
Tears shining on your cheeks
Wishing for your own Mum
Who you hadn't seen in weeks

It formed when you came to me in the night
Answering my cries,
It formed when you got up and faced the day,
Giving smiles through tired eyes

Poems from the Pandemic

And though I may not remember it all,
I'll have strength and independence
That you'll have modelled for me
Through those months of perseverance

I hope you know this, Mumma -
I hope you will believe
That you should be so proud of
That first year, and all you achieved

One day, those old history books
That seemed to forget us
Will lay discarded, lost to time,
Their pages turned to dust

And what will live on in their place
Are the memories that you formed -
Those sacred, tender moments,
In the year that I was born

And though I will love others
As the years they will go by,
My first true love was you, Mumma,
In that year of you and I.

Pandemic Poem

You cry for me, your mother,
But I'm pining for my own -
It's been months now since I've seen her,
Aside from on my phone
And the walls are closing in on us,
Every day the same -
Mustering the energy,
Another song, another game

And I'm meant to be the big one,
The one who soothes and sings,
The one whose needs now come last,
No matter what life brings
And I'll never again be the baby,
Though I crave my mother's arms -
The touch of her hands, cool and soft,
My head held in her palms

Yet she's far away, my mother
And as the weeks progress
I miss her touch more and more
And you know her less and less
So we go on alone, my baby
And I wonder if, one day,
You'll grow into a woman
And miss me the same way

I look down at your tiny form,
Curled against my breast
Your little face serene and still
My arms, the place that you love best
And I realise I'm already that -
The mother that you crave -
So we'll go on alone, my babe,
And I'll keep on being brave.

To The Locked-Down Mums

This one is for the locked-down mums
Who did it on their own,
The ones who worked it out themselves,
Within the confines of their home
This one is for the pandemic mums,
The ones who felt alone,
The ones who craved to share their babe
In real life, not just over the phone

This one is for the mothers who
Existed between four walls,
Who stayed inside for months on end,
Their lives agonisingly stalled
This is for the mothers whose "village"
Went missing, far-far away,
Stretched across cities, states or seas
Or perhaps just the wrong LGA

And this one is for the mothers who made
All of the big decisions -
Who learned from mistakes and still carried on,
With minimal help or provisions,
The mothers who - once in a while, at least -
Had to get up and walk away,
Swallowing tears, sick with the fear
Of relentless day-after-day

And this one is for the families and friends
Who sent you the cards and flowers,
Who cried with you during a video call,
Who stayed on the phone for hours,
And this one is for the partners - oh my,
The ones who have your heart,
The helper, the saviour, who held you together
When you felt you were coming apart

And this one is for the babies who know
Very few people at all;
Hours spent alone with Mum
From dawn until nightfall -
Yes, it may seem like a shame right now
Just the two of you, together,
Yet your souls have intertwined so deep,
A bond to last forever

For the weary days and sleepless nights
Are lonely, hard and long,
Yet they've sparked a magic, deep in you
It'll make you resilient and strong
And while sometimes it might feel like
The load will never ease,
Your journey into into motherhood has
A fearsome legacy

For though it may not seem like much
(Did you really have a choice?)
These months were carving out
A brand new you, a brand new voice
And every move you questioned,
And every endless chore,
Were kindling for that fire in you
And soon, that fire will roar

And now, as you move through motherhood,
With everything you do
You're building on a foundation so strong
Because it was built by YOU
And as for that little babe,
Well, what better model have they,
Than the one who kept on showing up
To feed
To change
To soothe
To bathe
To hold them,
Day after day.

Acknowledgements

This book and my creative works were written on the unceded lands of the Ngunnawal people, traditional owners of the ACT region. It is my dear wish to acknowledge that this Country belongs to an ancestry of people who have been birthing and raising children for tens of thousands of years. I pay respect to their vast knowledge, experiences, and stories related to motherhood.

Putting together a book of this nature takes not only time, effort and planning, but precious encouragement. I am so grateful for the support and encouragement of my family during this process, in particular my dear love, Nick, who motivated me not only to produce this collection of poems but to be brave enough to first share my writing publicly. Thank you for believing in what could come from this little passion project, and for being my equal, partner and constant support through all stages of parenthood.

Enormous thanks to my dear colleague and designer Teresa for producing the beautiful cover and for her meticulous and patient work in preparing the manuscript for publication. A sincere thank-you also to my Mum and Dad for always being my self-described 'number-one fans', for giving the three of us the gift of education and for nurturing an appreciation of words and writing in me from such an early age. Thanks too to all of my family for supporting the creation of this book and my work, including my dear parents-in-law, who were with me on that special and fateful day when I launched the business and shared in my happy tears.

The biggest thanks, of course, needs to go to you—the tens of thousands of mothers out there who have supported my work and made all of this possible. It sounds like a cliché, but it is true that none of this would have happened if it wasn't for your incredibly valuable and appreciated encouragement, sharing and feedback in your response to my writing. Countless times I have been completely floored and humbled by the incredible stories of motherhood that I have been privileged to witness as a result of being part of this community. All of the times that I have been told, 'thank you for making me feel that I was not alone', I have wanted to repeat those words straight back, for it has been a precious comfort to know that the personal experiences I have disclosed in my writing were shared by so many others.

With sincere thanks and gratitude,
Sarah.

About the Author

Sarah was born and raised in the coastal town of Newcastle, NSW. She gained a teaching qualification there and spent seven years teaching high school English and Humanities before having her first child in May, 2021.

In September 2021, Sarah began writing and sharing poetry in an attempt to navigate the early days of motherhood. Her Instagram page, Matrescent Muse, became popular with a large community of mothers and parents, and a subsequent website and online print store were launched in April, 2022. Today, Sarah's poetry is followed by an audience of almost 20,000 subscribers—a group of people with whom Sarah is honoured to be connected.

Sarah now lives in Canberra with her husband, daughter and a wayward old cat named Mr. Patches. After reconsidering her teaching career, she now works happily as an editor in the publishing industry. In any spare time that she can muster, she enjoys being outdoors with her family, watching TV series, reading fantasy or crime novels, visiting the coast, and eating just about any cuisine you could name.

This is her first book.

www.ingramcontent.com/pod-product-compliance
Lightning Source LLC
Chambersburg PA
CBHW020326010526
44107CB00054B/1998